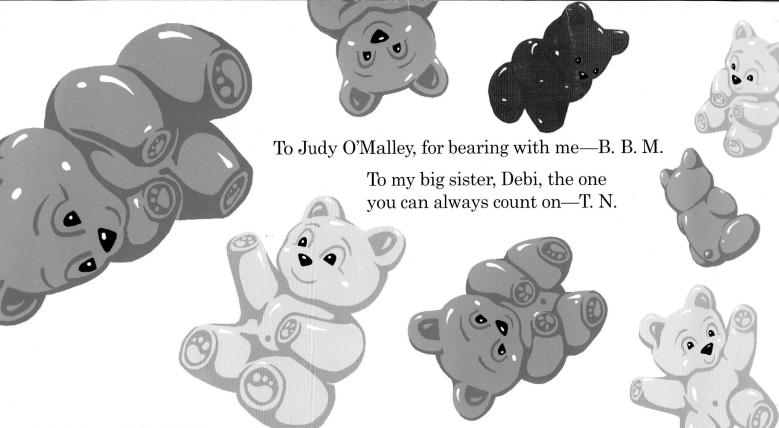

To Judy O'Malley, for bearing with me—B. B. M.

To my big sister, Debi, the one
you can always count on—T. N.

...yright © 2010 by Barbara Barbieri McGrath
...ions copyright © 2010 by Tim Nihoff
...s reserved, including the right of reproduction
... or in part in any form. Charlesbridge
...phon are registered trademarks of
...ridge Publishing, Inc.

...d by Charlesbridge
... Street
...wn, MA 02472
...6-0329
...arlesbridge.com

...in China
...9 8 7 6 5 4 3 2 1
...9 8 7 6 5 4 3 2 1

Library of Congress Cataloging-in-Publication Data
McGrath, Barbara Barbieri, 1954–
   Teddy bear counting / Barbara Barbieri McGrath ;
illustrated by Tim Nihoff.
       p. cm.
   Summary: Teddy bears introduce numbers from one to
twelve, as well as colors and shapes.
   ISBN 978-1-58089-215-5 (reinforced for library use)
   ISBN 978-1-58089-216-2 (softcover)
[1. Stories in rhyme. 2. Teddy bears—Fiction. 3. Counting.
4. Shape. 5. Color.] I. Nihoff, Tim, ill.
II. Title.
PZ8.3.M459584Te 2010
[E]—dc22   2008025339

Illustrations hand drawn digitally in Adobe Photoshop
Display type set in Animated Gothic and
   text type set in Century Schoolbook
Color separations by Chroma Graphics, Singapore
Manufactured by Regent Publishing Services, Hong Kon...
Printed September 2009 in ShenZhen, Guangdong, Chin...
Production supervision by Brian G. Walker
Designed by Susan Mallory Sherman

McGrath Math

TEDDY BEAR
COUNTING

Barbara Barbieri McGr

Illustrated by Tim Nil

Charlesbri

Bears tumble in.

Get ready, get set.
This counting book is
the most playful yet!

Bears say their colors.

It's easy to do.

"I'm red!"   "And I'm yellow!"

"I'm green!"

"Well, I'm blue!"

1

First is one red.

Yellow makes two.

A green bear is three.

Count four with this blue.

4

One red marches in

5

to make five bears in all.

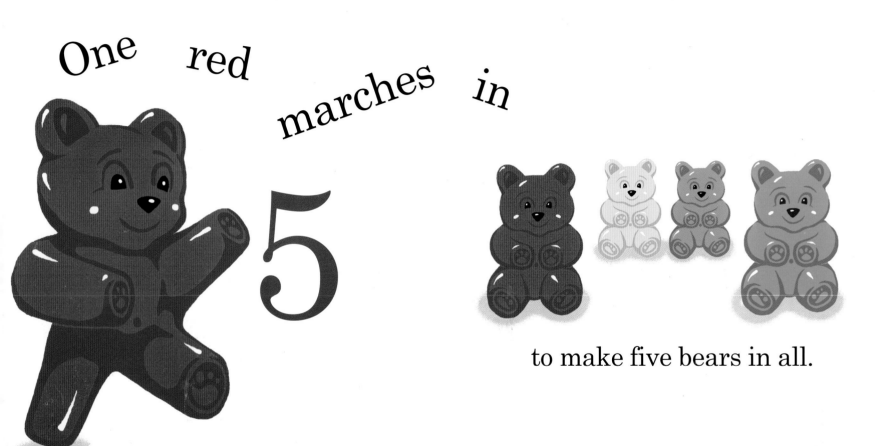

When yellow joins, too,

six teddies sit tall.

A green one arrives.
Seven now form a group.

7

Then a blue comes along,

making eight in the troop.

8

One bear cartwheels in
to make nine in the line.

9

Another drops by,
and ten teddies look fine.

10

Ten teddies line up,

then bend low to bow.

11

To count to eleven
add one teddy now.

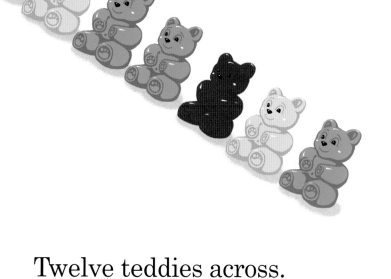

Add one more blue.

Now what can be seen?

Twelve teddies across.

Are there more red or green?

12

A set of twelve teddies

makes a rainbow for you.

Six bears can choose partners—

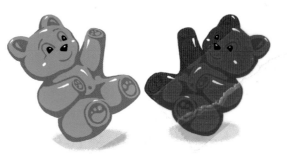

$2+2+2+2+2+2=12$

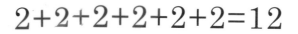

that's six sets of two.

The bears move around

and make three sets of four.

Count up how many:

just twelve and no more.

$$4+4+4=12$$

Teddies all dancing

make four sets of three,

and still only twelve

are all we can see.

$3+3+3+3=12$

Two sets of six say,
"How do you do?"

$6+6=12$

Since that went so well,
they try something new.

Bears hop,

skip, and jump,

and fly through the air.

When they all land

they make a big square.

The bears shape a circle

that goes round and round.

Can a circle's beginning ever be found?

A triangle's next

before these bears stop.

They give it three sides, with one bear on the top!

One bear of each color

won't risk being late.

Four bears have to go.

That leaves only eight.

$$12-4=8$$

More teddies are leaving.

It's bear moving day.

With places to go,

two more walk away.

$$8-2=6$$

Six bears remain

with little to do.

Say so long to four. . . .

We're left with just two.

 6−4=2

One little teddy

runs away fast.

Say hello to the bear
who chose to be last.

2−1=1

The bear stands alone.

What a brave little hero.

When he trots away,

there are none. That means zero!

0

$$1-1=0$$

Bye, counting bears.
They're gone now, but when
the teddies come back, they'll all play again!

The bears had great fun. They tried something new.
To help them remember, let's have a review!

COLORS SHAPES NUMBERS

red

yellow

green

blue

square

circle

triangle

1	one	5	five	9	nine
2	two	6	six	10	ten
3	three	7	seven	11	eleven
4	four	8	eight	12	twelve

SETS OF TWELVE

1 set

2 sets

3 sets

4 sets

6 sets